rly
to

Hockey

Great Moments, Records, and Facts

by Teddy Borth

ABDO
GREAT SPORTS
Kids

abdopublishing.com

Published by Abdo Kids, a division of ABDO, PO Box 398166, Minneapolis, Minnesota 55439.

Copyright © 2015 by Abdo Consulting Group, Inc. International copyrights reserved in all countries. No part of this book may be reproduced in any form without written permission from the publisher.

Printed in the United States of America, North Mankato, Minnesota.

102014

012015

 THIS BOOK CONTAINS RECYCLED MATERIALS

Photo Credits: AP Images, Corbis, iStock, Shutterstock, © KUCO / Shutterstock.com p.5

Production Contributors: Teddy Borth, Jennie Forsberg, Grace Hansen

Design Contributors: Laura Rask, Dorothy Toth

Library of Congress Control Number: 2014943663

Cataloging-in-Publication Data

Borth, Teddy.

 Hockey : great moments, records, and facts / Teddy Borth.

   p. cm. -- (Great sports)

ISBN 978-1-62970-691-7 (lib. bdg.)

Includes bibliographical references and index.

1. Hockey--Juvenile literature.   I. Title.

796.962--dc23

                  2014943663

Table of Contents

Hockey

Hockey started in the 1700s.

Rules were written in 1877.

There were only 7 rules.

5

The Rink

Canada has the most **rinks**. It has more than 2,500 indoor rinks. It has about 5,000 outdoor rinks.

Great Records

Wayne Gretzky is called "The Great One." He holds many records. He scored 894 goals. That is more than any player.

Glenn Hall is named "Mr. Goalie."

He played 502 games in a row.

He played without a mask.

Players can get **penalties**.
They have to sit in the penalty
box. Tiger Williams has the
most minutes in the box.
He sat for 3,966 minutes.

13

Miracle on Ice

It is the 1980 **Olympics**. The **Soviet Union** is picked to win. They are strong. They are winning every game. People think Team USA cannot win.

USA scores twice in the 3rd period. They have a 1-point lead. The **Soviets** attack. USA holds strong for 10 minutes. The Soviets are not able to score again. USA beats the Soviets!

17

Bobby Orr Takes Flight

The Bruins can win the 1970 **Stanley Cup**. They are playing the Blues. The game is tied 3–3. It goes to overtime. Bobby Orr gets a pass from his teammate.

19

He is tripped as he shoots.

He still scores the winning goal!

Orr flying becomes historic.

A monument was made to
remember it.

21

More Facts

- The fastest puck shot on record is 114 miles per hour (183 km/h).

- The NHL began in 1917 with only six teams. The teams were Boston, Chicago, Detroit, New York, Montreal, and Toronto.

- Teams and players who have won the **Stanley Cup** are written on the Cup itself. There are a few spelling errors on the Cup. This includes Boston being spelled as "Bqstqn," Maple Leaves as "Maple Leaes," and Islanders as "Ilanders."

Glossary

goalie – a player who stops the puck from going into the net.

Olympics – a sports event where teams around the world play each other. Winter games are held every four years.

penalty – a payment for breaking the rules. In hockey, this means sitting in a penalty box. The team then plays one person short to make up for breaking the rules.

rink – an area of ice for skating and playing hockey.

Soviet Union - a country from 1922 to 1991. It was where Russia is today.

Stanley Cup – The prize given to the best NHL team at the end of the season.

23

Index

abdokids.com

Use this code to log on to abdokids.com and access crafts, games, videos, and more!

Abdo Kids Code:
GHK6917